Is Daddy Coming Back in a Minute?

Explaining (sudden) death in words very young children can understand

Elke and Alex Barber

Illustrations by Anna Jarvis

Jessica Kingsley *Publishers*
London and Philadelphia

From us...

To Daddy

I love you,
I will always miss you
and never forget you.

Alex xxx

For Alex and Olivia
Love you always, xxx,
Mummy and Daddy in the Sky

For Mart - thanks for sharing
your short life with us. xxx

And for all you Little Ones,
who miss somebody terribly
and are trying to understand
- you are not alone.

Big hugs, xxx,
Elke, Alex and Olivia

For Lucy, Matthew,
Ella and Amelia,
in loving memory
of Simon.

Anna xx

...and from some of our amazing crowdfunders. xx

In memory of
"The Best Daddy in the World",
who died when his darlings were
5 years, 3 years and 4 days old.

We miss you every day.

Love Lucy, Matthew,
Ella and Amelia xxx

For Christian Nolan
and Niall Geldard.

Much-loved dads,
missed every day by
Max, Jessye,
Sophie and Hannah

xxxx

To Thomas

This is a special book
for a special lovely boy.

Lots of love,
Daddy xxx

September 2012

In memory of Martin,
a great friend, who is
always in our hearts
and never forgotten,
as we watch his two
beautiful and wonderfully
cheeky children growing
a little more like him
every day.

;o) Richard & Zoe X

In memory of Darren,
father to Jake (6)
and Harvey (3).

We cherish our memories,
you live on in our hearts.

xxx Kirsty

For Gavin,
a wonderful father
to Isaac and Clo,
who also lost their
daddy when they
were far too young.

Charlie X

Hi, I am Alex.

I am
(one...two...)
three
years old!

Daddy and I are going on a boys' weekend.
Just me and him.

No girls allowed!

My little sister Olivia and Mummy are staying at home.

We go on a black train with real steam coming out...

...and a boat, which takes us across a big lake.

We eat ham and pineapple pizza...

...and Daddy buys me ice-cream, which is just yummy!

The next morning, we have bacon sandwiches for breakfast. With tomato sauce.

Yum!

Suddenly, Daddy feels a bit poorly.

He says, "I need help, Alex. Please go and get a neighbour."

I go out, but there isn't anybody there.

So I go a bit further...

...until I find someone.

When I get back I say, "Daddy, I went a bit further!"

Daddy smiles at me and says, "Good lad."

Then the ambulance comes
with its flashing lights.
It is really noisy.

Daddy has to go to hospital.

I don't want him to go...

I play with the holiday park owners' pet lamb for ages.
Suddenly I see Mummy, carrying my toy ambulance.

I shout, "Oi! No girls allowed!"

Mummy smiles at me.

"Is Daddy coming back in a minute?" I ask.

Mummy kneels down and holds my ear to her chest.

"Can you hear that?" she asks.
I can hear a funny

bump

bump

bump.

"That's a **heart**," says Mummy.
"Everybody has got one.

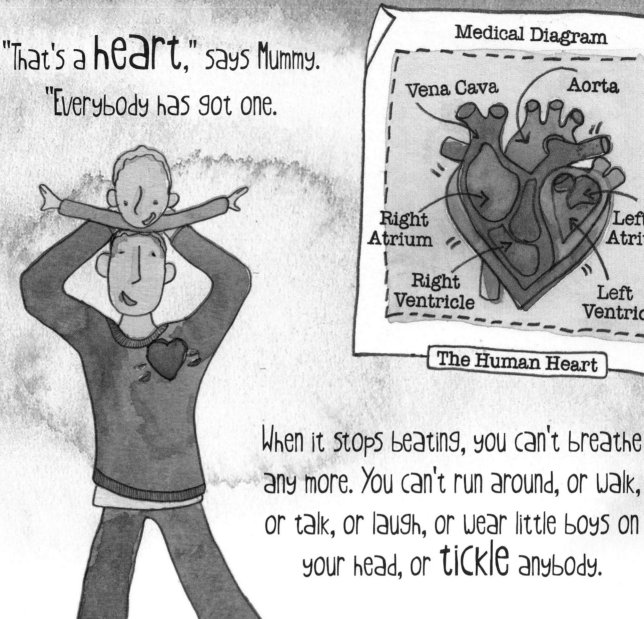

Medical Diagram

Vena Cava

Aorta

Right Atrium

Left Atrium

Right Ventricle

Left Ventricle

The Human Heart

When it stops beating, you can't breathe any more. You can't run around, or walk, or talk, or laugh, or wear little boys on your head, or **tickle** anybody.

Daddy's heart has stopped beating, and he is never coming back."

"Has he gone to work?" I ask.

Mummy starts to cry a little and says,
"No, Alex, he has not gone to work. His heart has
stopped beating, and he died. Daddy can't use his
body any more, and he is never coming back."

"But where is he?" I ask.

"Well," says Mummy, "some people like
to think of dead people as up in the sky.
They could be a cloud.
Or a star."

"But I don't want
Daddy to be a star!"
I cry.

"I want him to **come back down!**"

"He would like to, Alex,"
says Mummy, "but he can't.
His body has stopped working,
and he can never come back."

"But Mummy, did he say 'Please'?"

"Yes, Alex, he said 'Please'."

"But did he say 'Please, please, please, I need to go and see my little boy!'?"

"Yes, Alex, he did."

"But Mummy... did he say, 'Excuse me, please'?"

"Yes. He said 'Excuse me, please'.
But the ambulance people couldn't fix him.
His body stopped working and he died."

"The ambulance people couldn't fix my Daddy?"

"No, Alex. They did their very best, but sometimes people
are so badly hurt or broken, they can't be fixed.
Not even by ambulance people."

"But Mummy," I ask, "what if I hadn't found help?
Would Daddy still be okay?"

"No, Alex," says Mummy. "He would just have died where he was,
without the ambulance people to look after him.

It is not your fault that Daddy died.

You did a great job finding help, and I am very proud of you."

"But will he never come back?" I ask.

Mummy gives me a big hug and says,
"No, Alex. But we can talk about him every day
and always remember how much he loved us,
and that he didn't want to go."

The next few days are very busy.
Lots of people come to our house,
and the phone rings all the time.

Mummy says, "Tomorrow we are going to a place
where lots of people will talk about Daddy.
It is called a crematorium."

"Will they cry?" I ask.

"Yes, they probably will," says Mummy.

"Why?" I ask.

"Because they were all Daddy's friends,
and, just like us, they are very sad
that Daddy died and can't come back."

"Okay," I say.

When we get to the crematorium, there are **lots** of people. Just like Mummy said.

I play toy cars with my auntie. Mummy, Grandpa, and lots of Daddy's friends tell funny stories about Daddy.

At night, in bed, I say,
"Mummy... Will YOU have to die?"

"Yes," says Mummy,
"everybody has to die.

But most people won't die
until they are VERY old."

0
years

2
years

5
years

10
years

20
years

"Even older than
Granny and Grandpa?" I ask.

Mummy smiles.

"Yes, Alex. Even older
than Granny and Grandpa."

40
years

70
years

110
years

dead

"Who will look after me when YOU die, Mummy?"

"Well, hopefully I won't die until I am very old and you are all grown up."

"But what if you do?" I ask.

"If I die before you are big enough to look after yourself, Auntie Silke will."

"But what if She dies?"

"Then Oma and Opa will look after you."

"But what if they die?"

So we sit down and write a list
of all the people we love
very much, who would
look after me
if Mummy died.

"But Mummy...
How many more sleeps until **I have to die?**" I ask.

Mummy thinks for a bit,
and then she says,

"I know.
Let's go to the beach!"

We stay there **all day**
and collect shells.

When it starts to get dark, we count all the shells we collected.
Mummy needs to help me, because I don't know all
the numbers - there are SO many!

Mummy says, "See all these shells?

This is still a tiny number compared to the number
of sleeps most people have before they die."

"Wow...

...that IS...

...a lot of sleeps," I say.

Now I am (one...two...three...) **four** years old!

For my birthday, I am having a monster party.
I am **really** excited!

Sometimes I still have bad dreams and worries, so I tell people about them. Usually Mummy. Or my friends, or my teachers.

We all miss Daddy very much, and wish he could come back.
We talk about him every day.
But Mummy, Olivia and I still have lots of fun together.

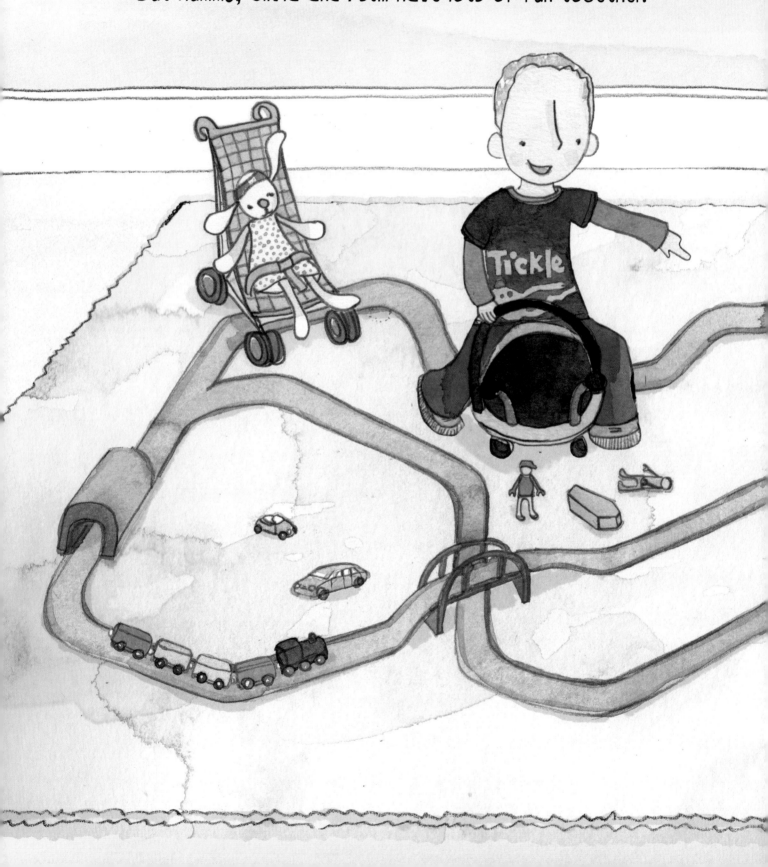

Mummy always says, "It's OKAY to be SAD, but it's okay to be HAPPY, too." And we are.

RIP Mart
20 July 1974
–
22 April 2009